100 Amazing Facts About Norway

A Collection of Amazing Facts About Norway

Introduction

Welcome to "100 Amazing Facts About Norway for Smart Kids"! Discover a land where fjords stretch like fingers into the sea, northern lights paint the sky, and trolls hide in the mountains. From Viking legends to modern-day innovations, Norway's story is filled with wonder and adventure. Get ready to explore this magical country and uncover its secrets! Through fascinating facts and captivating tales, you'll journey from historic castles to snowy peaks, learning why Norway is a land that captures hearts and imaginations alike.

Chapter 1: Introduction to Norway

Fact 1: Geography of Norway

Fact 2: Population and Demographics

Fact 3: Official Language

Fact 4: Currency and Economy

Fact 5: National Symbols

Fact 1: Geography of Norway

Norway is located in Northern Europe, sharing borders with Sweden, Finland, and Russia. It's renowned for its stunning natural landscapes, including majestic fjords, rugged coastlines, and expansive mountain ranges. The country spans a long, narrow stretch of land, stretching from the North Sea to the Arctic Ocean, making it one of the longest countries in Europe.

Fact 2: Population and Demographics

Norway has a population of around 5.4 million people. The majority of the population lives in the southern part of the country, particularly in urban areas such as Oslo, Bergen, and Stavanger. Norway is known for its high standard of living, extensive social welfare system, and commitment to equality. The country also has a diverse population, with a growing number of immigrants and a significant Sami indigenous community in the northern regions.

Fact 3: Official Language

The official language of Norway is Norwegian, which has two written forms: Bokmål and Nynorsk. Bokmål is the most widely used, particularly in urban areas, while Nynorsk is more commonly used in rural regions and among certain communities. Additionally, the Sami languages, spoken by the indigenous Sami people, have official status in certain municipalities in Northern Norway.

Fact 4: Currency and Economy

The currency of Norway is the Norwegian Krone (NOK), often symbolized as "kr". Norway has a mixed economy with a combination of free market activity and significant government involvement. It is one of the world's wealthiest countries, largely due to its rich natural resources, including oil and gas. Norway's economy also benefits from industries such as shipping, fishing, and renewable energy.

Fact 5: National Symbols

Norway's national symbols reflect its history, culture, and natural beauty. The national flag features a red background with a blue cross outlined in white, symbolizing freedom and independence. The lion is a prominent symbol in Norwegian heraldry, often associated with the country's monarchy and historical significance. The national flower of Norway is the purple heather, and the white-throated dipper is the national bird.

Chapter 2: History of Norway

Fact 6: Viking Era

Fact 7: The Unification of Norway

Fact 8: The Kalmar Union

Fact 9: Independence in 1905

Fact 10: Norway during World War II

Fact 6: Viking Era

The Viking Era, spanning from around 800 to 1050 AD, was a defining period in Norwegian history. Norwegian Vikings were renowned seafarers, explorers, and traders who traveled as far as North America, Russia, and the Middle East. The Viking legacy is still evident in Norway's cultural traditions, folklore, and archaeological sites.

Fact 7: The Unification of Norway

The unification of Norway is traditionally attributed to King Harald Fairhair, who is said to have unified the various petty kingdoms around 872 AD after the Battle of Hafrsfjord. The unification process was gradual, and subsequent kings continued to strengthen and expand their control over the region, laying the foundation for the modern nation of Norway.

Fact 8: The Kalmar Union

The Kalmar Union was a series of personal unions that united the kingdoms of Denmark, Norway, and Sweden under a single monarch from 1397 to 1523. However, internal conflicts and differing interests among the member kingdoms led to its eventual dissolution. Norway remained in a union with Denmark until 1814.

Fact 9: Independence in 1905

Norway gained its independence from Sweden in 1905 following a peaceful dissolution of the union between the two countries. A national referendum showed overwhelming support for independence, and Prince Carl of Denmark was invited to become King Haakon VII of Norway. This marked the establishment of Norway as a fully sovereign and independent nation.

Fact 10: Norway during World War II

During World War II, Norway was occupied by Nazi Germany from 1940 to 1945. The invasion began on April 9, 1940, and the Norwegian government went into exile in London. Despite the occupation, there was significant resistance from Norwegian citizens, including organized resistance groups and efforts to protect Jews and other persecuted individuals.

- **Chapter 3: Culture and Traditions**

- Fact 11: Norwegian Folk Music

- Fact 12: Traditional Clothing (Bunad)

- Fact 13: National Holidays and Festivals

- Fact 14: Norwegian Cuisine

- Fact 15: Literature and Storytelling

Fact 11: Norwegian Folk Music

Norwegian folk music is an integral part of the country's cultural heritage, characterized by traditional instruments like the Hardanger fiddle and langeleik. This music often accompanies dances and celebrations, and its themes are deeply rooted in nature, folklore, and rural life. The unique sounds of Norwegian folk music continue to influence modern Norwegian music and are celebrated at various festivals.

Fact 12: Traditional Clothing (Bunad)

The Bunad is traditional Norwegian clothing, often worn during special occasions such as weddings, holidays, and national celebrations. Each region in Norway has its own distinctive Bunad design, featuring intricate embroidery, vibrant colors, and unique accessories. The Bunad is a symbol of Norwegian identity and pride, showcasing the country's rich textile heritage.

Fact 13: National Holidays and Festivals

Norway has several national holidays and festivals that reflect its culture and traditions. The most significant is Constitution Day on May 17th, celebrated with parades, traditional music, and public gatherings. Other important festivals include Christmas, which features unique Norwegian customs, and Midsummer (St. Hans), celebrated with bonfires and outdoor festivities.

Fact 14: Norwegian Cuisine

Norwegian cuisine is known for its use of fresh, locally sourced ingredients, with a strong emphasis on seafood. Traditional dishes include gravlaks (cured salmon), rakfisk (fermented fish), and fårikål (mutton and cabbage stew). Norway is also famous for its dairy products, breads, and pastries. Modern Norwegian cuisine blends traditional recipes with contemporary culinary techniques.

Fact 15: Literature and Storytelling

Norwegian literature has a rich history, with famous writers such as Henrik Ibsen and Knut Hamsun making significant contributions to world literature. Storytelling is an important aspect of Norwegian culture, with a tradition of folk tales featuring mythical creatures like trolls and huldra. Contemporary Norwegian authors continue to gain international acclaim, adding to the country's vibrant literary scene.

Chapter 4: Nature and Wildlife

Fact 16: Fjords and Glaciers

Norway is famous for its breathtaking fjords and glaciers, which are among the country's most iconic natural features. The fjords, created by ancient glacial activity, are deep, narrow inlets surrounded by steep cliffs and lush landscapes. The Sognefjord, the longest and deepest fjord in Norway, and the Geirangerfjord are particularly renowned.

Fact 17: Arctic Wildlife

Norway's Arctic regions, including Svalbard and the northern mainland, are home to a diverse array of wildlife. Visitors can encounter polar bears, Arctic foxes, reindeer, and walruses in their natural habitats. Efforts are made to preserve these fragile environments and protect the wildlife that inhabits them.

Fact 18: National Parks

Norway boasts numerous national parks that showcase its diverse landscapes and wildlife. Some of the most notable include Jotunheimen, known for its towering peaks and glaciers; Hardangervidda, the largest plateau in Europe; and Rondane, home to wild reindeer herds. These parks offer extensive hiking trails, scenic vistas, and opportunities for outdoor activities.

Fact 19: Bird Watching in Norway

Norway is a paradise for bird watchers, with its varied habitats supporting a wide range of bird species. The coastal areas, wetlands, and forests are particularly rich in birdlife. The Varanger Peninsula in the north is famous for its Arctic bird species, while the island of Runde in the west hosts large colonies of seabirds, including puffins and kittiwakes.

Fact 20: Marine Life

Norway's extensive coastline and cold, nutrient-rich waters support a diverse marine ecosystem. The waters are home to various species of fish, including cod, herring, and mackerel, which are vital to the country's fishing industry. Whale watching tours are popular, particularly in the regions of Tromsø and Andenes, where visitors can observe these majestic creatures up close.

Chapter 5: Funny Facts

- Fact 21: Lutefisk Christmas Tradition

- Fact 22: Kvikk Lunsj Adventures

- Fact 23: Weather Wisdom

- Fact 24: Rjukan's Sunny Solution

- Fact 25: Sir Nils Olav, the Penguin Knight

Fact 21: Lutefisk Christmas Tradition

Norwegians have a unique Christmas Eve tradition involving "Lutefisk," a dish made from dried whitefish treated with lye. Despite its strong smell, it's a cherished part of their festive season, enjoyed with potatoes, bacon, and peas. Families gather around tables adorned with candles and festive decorations, sharing stories and laughter as they enjoy this traditional dish together.

Fact 22: Kvikk Lunsj Adventures

In Norway, outdoor adventures are incomplete without "Kvikk Lunsj," a chocolate bar akin to Kit-Kat. This treat is a staple in hiking backpacks and picnic baskets, offering a sweet boost during excursions through Norway's stunning landscapes. It's not just a snack; it's a cultural icon that fuels Norwegians as they explore fjords, mountains, and forests, with each "snap" of chocolate bringing a moment of delight.

Fact 23: Weather Wisdom

Norwegians famously say, "There's no such thing as bad weather, only bad clothing!" This humorous adage reflects their pragmatic approach to Norway's unpredictable climate. From sudden rain showers to snowstorms, Norwegians embrace the outdoors with proper gear and a resilient spirit. They take pride in their ability to adapt, turning even the most challenging weather into opportunities for outdoor fun and adventure.

Fact 24: Rjukan's Sunny Solution

Imagine a town so surrounded by mountains that it gets little sunlight in winter. That's Rjukan in Norway! To brighten their winters, engineers installed enormous mirrors on the mountainsides to reflect sunlight down into the town square. This innovative solution has become a unique attraction, drawing visitors intrigued by this quirky use of technology. The mirrors, known locally as "Solspeil," create a surreal spectacle as they track the sun's path across the sky, bringing warmth and light to the town below.

Fact 25: Sir Nils Olav, the Penguin Knight

Norway has a charming tradition of knighting animals. Meet Sir Nils Olav, a king penguin residing at the Edinburgh Zoo in Scotland. This distinguished bird holds an honorary knighthood bestowed by the Norwegian King's Guard, symbolizing the close ties between Norway and Scotland in a delightful and unexpected way. Sir Nils Olav is not just a penguin; he's a beloved ambassador, visited by dignitaries and tourists alike who marvel at his unique title and charming personality.

Chapter 6: Science and Innovation

- Fact 26: The Kon-Tiki Expedition

- Fact 27: Innovations in Oil and Gas

-

- Fact 28: Renewable Energy Initiatives

- Fact 29: Polar Research

- Fact 30: Advances in Maritime Technology

Fact 26: The Kon-Tiki Expedition

The Kon-Tiki expedition, led by Norwegian adventurer Thor Heyerdahl in 1947, involved sailing a balsa wood raft from South America to the Polynesian islands to demonstrate the feasibility of ancient transoceanic contact. This daring journey sparked international interest and contributed significantly to our understanding of early maritime history and migration.

Fact 27: Innovations in Oil and Gas

Norway has been a pioneer in offshore oil and gas exploration and technology. The discovery of oil in the North Sea in the 1960s propelled Norway into becoming one of the world's largest oil exporters. Norwegian innovations in subsea technology, safety protocols, and environmental stewardship have set global standards in the oil and gas industry.

Fact 28: Renewable Energy Initiatives

Norway is committed to sustainable development and has invested heavily in renewable energy initiatives, particularly hydropower. Hydropower accounts for the majority of Norway's electricity production, making it one of the greenest countries in the world. Additionally, Norway is exploring wind, solar, and bioenergy sources to further reduce its carbon footprint and promote clean energy solutions.

Fact 29: Polar Research

Norway is a leader in polar research, conducting scientific expeditions and maintaining research stations in the Arctic and Antarctic regions. Norwegian scientists study climate change, marine biology, glaciology, and geology to better understand polar ecosystems and their global impact. Collaborative efforts with international partners contribute to advancing polar science and environmental conservation.

Fact 30: Advances in Maritime Technology

Norwegian shipbuilders and marine engineers have developed state-of-the-art vessels equipped with cutting-edge navigation systems, eco-friendly propulsion technologies, and safety features. Norway's expertise extends to offshore engineering, aquaculture, and marine resource management, positioning the country as a global leader in maritime innovation.

Chapter 7: Sports and Recreation

- Fact 31: Winter Sports Popularity

- Fact 32: Famous Norwegian Athletes

- Fact 33: Outdoor Activities

- Fact 34: Traditional Sports

- Fact 35: Skiing Culture

Fact 31: Winter Sports Popularity

Winter sports hold a special place in Norwegian culture, with activities like skiing, ice skating, and snowboarding enjoyed by people of all ages. Norwegians actively participate in skiing events, biathlon, and ski jumping, both competitively and recreationally, making winter sports a vital part of national identity.

Fact 32: Famous Norwegian Athletes

Norway has produced numerous world-class athletes who excel in various sports. Athletes like Ole Einar Bjørndalen (biathlon), Marit Bjørgen (cross-country skiing), and Aksel Lund Svindal (alpine skiing) have achieved international recognition and Olympic success, inspiring future generations with their athletic prowess and dedication.

Fact 33: Outdoor Activities

Norway's diverse landscapes offer ample opportunities for outdoor activities year-round. From hiking and fishing in the fjords to kayaking and rafting in the rivers, outdoor enthusiasts can explore Norway's natural beauty through a wide range of recreational pursuits.

Fact 34: Traditional Sports

Traditional Norwegian sports such as Kubb (a wooden block throwing game), Hnefatafl (a strategic board game), and Bandy (a form of ice hockey) reflect the country's cultural heritage and community spirit. These sports are often played at local gatherings and festivals, preserving Norwegian traditions and fostering camaraderie among participants.

Fact 35: Skiing Culture

Skiing is deeply ingrained in Norwegian culture, with a history dating back thousands of years. Norwegians pioneered modern skiing techniques and equipment, influencing the development of skiing as a sport worldwide. Today, cross-country skiing and alpine skiing are popular activities enjoyed by Norwegians of all ages, with world-class facilities and events hosted throughout the country.

Chapter 8: Education and Learning

- Fact 36: Education System

- Fact 37: Prominent Universities

- Fact 38: Literacy Rates

- Fact 39: Learning Norwegian

- Fact 40: Children's Literature

Fact 36: Education System

Norway's education system is known for its high quality and emphasis on equal access to education. It is based on the principles of inclusive education, with public education being free and compulsory for children aged 6 to 16. The system promotes lifelong learning and encourages students to pursue higher education or vocational training.

Fact 37: Prominent Universities

Norway is home to several prominent universities known for their academic excellence and research contributions. Institutions like the University of Oslo, NTNU (Norwegian University of Science and Technology), and the University of Bergen attract students from around the world with their diverse programs and innovative research initiatives.

Fact 38: Literacy Rates

Norway boasts one of the highest literacy rates in the world, with virtually all adults being literate. The country places a strong emphasis on education and literacy from an early age, ensuring that individuals have the skills and knowledge to participate fully in society and contribute to Norway's economic and cultural development.

Fact 39: Learning Norwegian

Learning Norwegian is important for both residents and newcomers to Norway. While English is widely spoken, Norwegian is the official language and essential for integration into Norwegian society. Language courses and resources are available to help individuals learn Norwegian effectively, facilitating communication and cultural understanding.

Fact 40: Children's Literature

Norwegian children's literature is rich in storytelling and cultural significance. Authors like Thorbjørn Egner, known for "Karius and Baktus" and "Hakkebakke Forest," and Anne-Cath. Vestly, with her "Eight Children" series, have captivated generations of young readers with imaginative tales and memorable characters. Children's literature plays a vital role in language development and fostering a love for reading among Norwegian youth.

Chapter 9: Places to Visit

- Fact 41: The Lofoten Islands

- Fact 42: The Viking Ship Museum

- Fact 43: Bryggen in Bergen

- Fact 44: The North Cape

- Fact 45: Oslo Opera House

Fact 41: The Lofoten Islands

The Lofoten Islands are a stunning archipelago known for their dramatic landscapes, picturesque fishing villages, and vibrant wildlife. Located above the Arctic Circle, they offer breathtaking scenery with towering mountains, deep fjords, and sandy beaches. Visitors can enjoy outdoor activities like hiking, fishing, kayaking, and even surfing, as well as witness the mesmerizing Northern Lights.

Fact 42: The Viking Ship Museum

The Viking Ship Museum in Oslo is a must-visit for history enthusiasts. It houses well-preserved Viking ships and artifacts discovered in burial mounds around the Oslo Fjord. The Oseberg, Gokstad, and Tune ships are the highlights, offering a glimpse into the seafaring life and craftsmanship of the Vikings. The museum also features exhibits on Viking culture and daily life.

Fact 43: Bryggen in Bergen

Bryggen is a historic wharf in Bergen that showcases the city's Hanseatic heritage. The colorful wooden buildings, dating back to the 14th century, line the waterfront and are a testament to Bergen's role as a major trading center. Visitors can explore the narrow alleyways, visit artisan shops, and learn about the history of the Hanseatic League at the Bryggen Museum.

Fact 44: The North Cape

The North Cape (Nordkapp) is one of the northernmost points in Europe, offering spectacular views of the Arctic Ocean. Located on the island of Magerøya, it features a visitor center with exhibits on the region's history, climate, and wildlife. The North Cape is a popular destination to experience the Midnight Sun during summer or the Northern Lights during winter.

Fact 45: Oslo Opera House

The Oslo Opera House is an architectural marvel and cultural landmark in Norway's capital. Located at the waterfront of the Oslo Fjord, its striking design features a sloping marble roof that visitors can walk on, offering panoramic views of the city and harbor. The opera house hosts a variety of performances, including opera, ballet, and concerts, and provides guided tours to explore its impressive interior and backstage areas.

Chapter 10: Travel Tips

- Fact 46: Best Time to Visit Norway

- Fact 47: Transportation in Norway

- Fact 48: Budget Travel Tips

- Fact 49: Safety Tips for Travelers

- Fact 50: Cultural Etiquette

Fact 46: Best Time to Visit Norway

The best time to visit Norway depends on what you want to experience. For mild weather and outdoor activities, the summer months of June to August are ideal, with long days and the Midnight Sun in the north. Winter, from December to February, is perfect for skiing and seeing the Northern Lights. Spring and autumn offer fewer crowds and stunning natural scenery with blooming flowers or autumn colors.

Fact 47: Transportation in Norway

Norway has an efficient and extensive transportation network. Trains, buses, and ferries connect major cities and remote areas, making travel convenient. The scenic train routes, like the Bergen Line, offer breathtaking views of Norway's landscapes. In cities, public transportation is reliable, and renting a car provides flexibility to explore the countryside.

Fact 48: Budget Travel Tips

Traveling in Norway can be expensive, but there are ways to save money. Consider visiting during the off-season for lower accommodation prices. Use public transportation or rent a car for group travel. Take advantage of the abundant nature for free activities like hiking and exploring national parks. Grocery stores offer affordable meals, and some accommodations have kitchens for self-catering.

Fact 49: Safety Tips for Travelers

Norway is one of the safest countries in the world, but travelers should still take basic precautions. Keep an eye on your belongings in crowded areas and use hotel safes for valuables. Be prepared for varying weather conditions, especially if exploring outdoors. Inform someone about your travel plans when venturing into remote areas and always follow local safety guidelines.

Fact 50: Cultural Etiquette

Understanding cultural etiquette will enhance your experience in Norway. Norwegians value punctuality, so be on time for appointments and social gatherings. Respect personal space and avoid interrupting conversations. It's customary to remove your shoes when entering someone's home. Learning a few basic Norwegian phrases is appreciated, even though many Norwegians speak English fluently.

Chapter 11: Famous Cities

- Fact 51: Oslo – The Capital
-

- Fact 52: Bergen – The Gateway to the Fjords

- Fact 53: Trondheim – Historical City

- Fact 54: Stavanger – Oil Capital 55.

- Fact 55: Tromsø – Gateway to the Arctic

Fact 51: Oslo – The Capital

Oslo, the capital of Norway, is a vibrant city known for its rich cultural scene, green spaces, and modern architecture. The city is home to notable landmarks like the Royal Palace, Vigeland Sculpture Park, and the modern Oslo Opera House. Oslo also offers numerous museums, including the Viking Ship Museum and the Munch Museum, and is a hub for Norwegian arts, politics, and commerce.

Fact 52: Bergen – The Gateway to the Fjords

Bergen, known as the "Gateway to the Fjords," is a picturesque city surrounded by mountains and fjords. Its historic Bryggen wharf reflects its Hanseatic trading past. Bergen is also famous for its vibrant cultural life, including the annual Bergen International Festival, and serves as a starting point for fjord cruises and hikes in the stunning surrounding landscapes.

Fact 53: Trondheim – Historical City

Trondheim, one of Norway's oldest cities, boasts a rich history and is home to the impressive Nidaros Cathedral, the northernmost medieval cathedral in the world. The city was once the Viking capital of Norway and continues to be a center of education and technology with the Norwegian University of Science and Technology (NTNU). Trondheim's charming old town, Bakklandet, features colorful wooden houses and cobblestone streets.

Fact 54: Stavanger – Oil Capital

Stavanger is often referred to as Norway's "Oil Capital" due to its significant role in the country's petroleum industry. The city is known for its modern amenities and historic charm, with attractions such as the Stavanger Cathedral and the Norwegian Petroleum Museum. Stavanger also serves as a gateway to the famous Pulpit Rock (Preikestolen), a popular hiking destination with stunning views over the Lysefjord.

Fact 55: Tromsø – Gateway to the Arctic

Tromsø, located above the Arctic Circle, is known as the "Gateway to the Arctic." It offers unique Arctic experiences, including the chance to see the Northern Lights and the Midnight Sun. The city is home to the Arctic Cathedral, the Polar Museum, and the Tromsø University Museum. Tromsø is also a starting point for Arctic expeditions and offers a range of outdoor activities like dog sledding and whale watching.

- **Chapter 12: Arts and Entertainment**

- Fact 56: Norwegian Cinema

- Fact 57: Popular Music Genres

- Fact 58: Theatre and Performing Arts

- Fact 59: Art Galleries and Museums

- Fact 60: Festivals and Events

Fact 56: Norwegian Cinema

Norwegian cinema has gained international recognition for its unique storytelling and high production quality. Films from Norway have showcased the country's cinematic talents. The Norwegian Film Institute supports the industry, and the annual Oslo International Film Festival celebrates both Norwegian and international films, contributing to the country's vibrant film culture.

Fact 57: Popular Music Genres

Norwegian music encompasses a wide range of genres, from traditional folk and classical to contemporary pop and black metal. Artists like A-ha brought Norwegian pop music to global fame, while bands like Mayhem and Dimmu Borgir are iconic in the black metal scene. The country also has a rich jazz tradition, with the Oslo Jazz Festival being a highlight of the music calendar.

Fact 58: Theatre and Performing Arts

Theatre and performing arts are integral to Norwegian culture. The National Theatre in Oslo is the country's leading venue for dramatic arts, staging both classic and contemporary plays. The Norwegian Opera & Ballet also offers world-class performances. Regional theaters and numerous festivals, such as the Bergen International Festival, showcase a variety of performing arts, from traditional dance to experimental theater.

Fact 59: Art Galleries and Museums

Norway is home to a wealth of art galleries and museums that celebrate its artistic heritage. The National Gallery in Oslo houses an extensive collection of Norwegian art, including works by Edvard Munch. The Astrup Fearnley Museum of Modern Art features contemporary international art. Throughout the country, smaller galleries and museums display local and historical art, reflecting Norway's diverse artistic landscape.

Fact 60: Festivals and Events

Norway hosts numerous festivals and events that celebrate its culture and arts. The Bergen International Festival is one of the largest arts festivals in the Nordic countries, offering music, dance, theater, and visual arts. The Norwegian Wood Festival in Oslo features major international and local music acts. Traditional events like the Sami Easter Festival in Kautokeino celebrate indigenous Sami culture with music, dance, and reindeer racing.

Chapter 13: Economy and Industry

- Fact 61: Oil and Gas Industry

- Fact 62: Fishing Industry

- Fact 63: Shipbuilding and Maritime Industry

- Fact 64: Technological Innovations

- Fact 65: Tourism Industry

Fact 61: Oil and Gas Industry

Norway's economy heavily relies on its oil and gas industry, which accounts for a significant portion of the country's GDP and exports. The discovery of oil in the North Sea during the late 1960s transformed Norway into one of the world's largest oil exporters. The government manages oil revenues through the Government Pension Fund Global, ensuring sustainable wealth distribution and economic stability.

Fact 62: Fishing Industry

The fishing industry is a cornerstone of Norway's economy, with the country being one of the world's leading exporters of seafood. Norway's extensive coastline and rich marine resources support a thriving fishing sector, producing high-quality fish like salmon, cod, and mackerel. Sustainable fishing practices and aquaculture are vital components of the industry, contributing to global food security and economic growth.

Fact 63: Shipbuilding and Maritime Industry

Norway has a long maritime tradition, with a robust shipbuilding and maritime industry. The country is renowned for constructing advanced vessels, including cruise ships, tankers, and offshore platforms. Norwegian maritime companies are leaders in developing cutting-edge technologies for marine navigation, safety, and environmental sustainability, reinforcing Norway's status as a global maritime hub.

Fact 64: Technological Innovations

Norway is at the forefront of technological innovations, particularly in sectors like renewable energy, telecommunications, and healthcare. The country invests heavily in research and development, fostering a vibrant tech industry. Innovations such as the world's first electric car ferry and advancements in telemedicine showcase Norway's commitment to leveraging technology for sustainable and efficient solutions.

Fact 65: Tourism Industry

The tourism industry in Norway is a growing sector, attracting millions of visitors annually. Tourists are drawn to Norway's natural beauty, including its fjords, Northern Lights, and mountains. Major cities like Oslo, Bergen, and Tromsø offer cultural and historical attractions. The tourism industry significantly contributes to the economy by providing employment opportunities and supporting local businesses across the country.

- **Chapter 14: Food and Cuisine**

- Fact 66: Traditional Norwegian Dishes

- Fact 67: Seafood Specialties

- Fact 68: Popular Desserts

- Fact 69: Food Markets 70.

- Fact 70: Modern Norwegian Cuisine

Fact 66: Traditional Norwegian Dishes

Traditional Norwegian cuisine is hearty and reflects the country's natural resources and history. Classic dishes include "raspeballer" (potato dumplings), "fårikål" (mutton and cabbage stew), and "lutefisk" (dried fish reconstituted in lye). These dishes are often enjoyed during specific seasons and festivals, showcasing Norway's culinary heritage.

Fact 67: Seafood Specialties

Norway's extensive coastline and rich marine life make seafood a staple in Norwegian cuisine. Fresh and cured fish like salmon, cod, and herring are central to many dishes. "Rakfisk" (fermented fish) and "klippfisk" (dried and salted cod) are popular traditional preparations, while seafood platters featuring shrimp, crab, and mussels are commonly enjoyed.

Fact 68: Popular Desserts

Norwegian desserts often feature berries, dairy, and spices. "Krumkake" (thin, crispy cookies), "riskrem" (rice pudding with whipped cream), and "multekrem" (cloudberries with whipped cream) are beloved sweets. "Kvæfjordkake," known as the world's best cake, combines meringue, almonds, and custard for a delightful treat.

Fact 69: Food Markets

Food markets in Norway offer a glimpse into the country's culinary diversity and local produce. The Mathallen in Oslo and the Fish Market in Bergen are popular destinations where visitors can sample fresh seafood, artisanal cheeses, cured meats, and other Norwegian specialties. These markets also feature food stalls and restaurants serving traditional and modern dishes.

Fact 70: Modern Norwegian Cuisine

Modern Norwegian cuisine blends traditional ingredients with contemporary techniques and international influences. Chefs focus on sustainability and local sourcing, creating innovative dishes that highlight Norway's natural bounty. Restaurants like Maaemo in Oslo, which has earned multiple Michelin stars, are at the forefront of this culinary revolution, offering unique and memorable dining experiences.

Chapter 15: Language and Communication

- Fact 71: Norwegian Language Facts

- Fact 72: Dialects in Norway

- Fact 73: Language Education

- Fact 74: Sign Language in Norway

- Fact 75: Common Norwegian Phrases

Fact 71: Norwegian Language Facts

The Norwegian language has two official written forms: Bokmål and Nynorsk. Bokmål is used by the majority of the population, while Nynorsk is prevalent in rural areas and western Norway. Both forms are taught in schools, and government documents are available in both. Norwegian belongs to the North Germanic language family, sharing similarities with Swedish and Danish, which makes these languages mutually intelligible to some extent.

Fact 72: Dialects in Norway

Norway has a wide variety of regional dialects that can vary significantly from one area to another. These dialects are often so distinct that they can be difficult for even native speakers to understand if they are not familiar with them. Despite this, dialects are an important part of local identity and culture, and Norwegians take pride in their linguistic diversity.

Fact 73: Language Education

Language education is highly valued in Norway. Norwegian children begin learning English at an early age, typically in primary school, making most Norwegians fluent in English. In addition to English, many students also learn other languages such as German, French, or Spanish. Schools emphasize the importance of multilingualism to prepare students for a globalized world.

Fact 74: Sign Language in Norway

Norwegian Sign Language (NSL) is recognized as an official language in Norway. It has its own unique grammar and vocabulary, distinct from spoken Norwegian. NSL is used by the deaf community and is taught in schools for the deaf. The government supports the use of NSL through various initiatives to ensure accessibility and inclusion for the deaf and hard-of-hearing population.

Fact 75: Common Norwegian Phrases

Common Norwegian Phrases Learning a few common Norwegian phrases can greatly enhance communication and show respect for the local culture. Some useful phrases include:

"Hei" (Hello)

"Takk" (Thank you)

"Ja" (Yes) and "Nei" (No)

"Hvordan har du det?" (How are you?)

These basic phrases can help visitors navigate everyday interactions and demonstrate an appreciation for the Norwegian language.

- **Chapter 16: Government and Politics**

- Fact 76: The Norwegian Constitution

- Fact 77: Political System

- .Fact 78: Role in International Organizations

- Fact 79: Human Rights Initiatives

- Fact 80: Environmental Policies

Fact 76: The Norwegian Constitution

The Norwegian Constitution, adopted on May 17, 1814, is one of the oldest constitutions still in use today. It established Norway as a constitutional monarchy and laid the foundation for democratic governance. The Constitution outlines the separation of powers among the executive, legislative, and judicial branches, ensuring a system of checks and balances to protect citizens' rights and freedoms.

Fact 77: Political System

Norway operates under a parliamentary system within the framework of a constitutional monarchy. The Storting, Norway's national parliament, is the supreme legislature, consisting of 169 elected members. The Prime Minister, appointed by the King, heads the government and is usually the leader of the majority party or coalition in the Storting. Norway's political landscape is characterized by multiple parties, often requiring coalition governments.

Fact 78: Role in International Organizations

Norway actively participates in various international organizations, playing a significant role in global diplomacy and development. It is a founding member of the United Nations and contributes to peacekeeping missions, humanitarian aid, and sustainable development initiatives. Norway is also a member of NATO and the European Free Trade Association (EFTA), promoting regional security and economic cooperation.

Fact 79: Human Rights Initiatives

Norway is known for its strong commitment to human rights, both domestically and internationally. The country advocates for gender equality, freedom of expression, and the protection of minority rights. Norway supports numerous global human rights initiatives and organizations, such as Amnesty International and Human Rights Watch, and provides substantial funding for human rights projects worldwide.

Fact 80: Environmental Policies

Norway is a global leader in environmental protection and sustainability. The country has implemented comprehensive policies to reduce greenhouse gas emissions, promote renewable energy, and protect natural habitats. Norway's government has committed to becoming carbon-neutral by 2030 and invests heavily in green technologies. Initiatives like the Green Tax Shift and extensive electric vehicle incentives reflect Norway's dedication to combating climate change.

- **Chapter 17: Festivals and Celebrations**

- Fact 81: National Day (17th of May)

- Fact 82: Sami National Day

- Fact 83: Christmas Traditions

- Fact 84: Easter Celebrations

- Fact 85: Midsummer Celebrations

Fact 81: National Day (17th of May)

Norway's National Day, celebrated on the 17th of May, marks the signing of the Norwegian Constitution in 1814. It is a day of patriotic celebration, featuring parades, traditional costumes (bunads), and public festivities. Children's parades, with schoolchildren marching through the streets waving flags, are a highlight of the day. This holiday fosters a strong sense of national pride and community.

Fact 82: Sami National Day

Sami National Day is celebrated on February 6th, commemorating the first Sami congress held in Trondheim in 1917. The Sami people, an indigenous group in Norway, Sweden, Finland, and Russia, celebrate with traditional music, dancing, and joik (a unique form of song). The day also includes cultural exhibitions, reindeer races, and events that highlight Sami heritage and rights.

Fact 83: Christmas Traditions

Christmas in Norway is a festive season rich in traditions. Celebrations begin with Advent, and many homes are decorated with candles, wreaths, and Christmas trees. "Julebord" (Christmas parties) are popular in the lead-up to Christmas. On Christmas Eve, families gather for a festive meal, often featuring dishes like ribbe (pork ribs) or pinnekjøtt (dried lamb ribs). The holiday also includes church services, gift-giving, and a visit from "Julenissen" (Santa Claus).

Fact 84: Easter Celebrations

Easter, or "Påske" in Norway, is a time for both religious observance and outdoor activities. Many Norwegians take advantage of the long holiday to go skiing in the mountains or relax in cabins. Traditional Easter foods include lamb, eggs, and a variety of pastries. Families often read crime novels, known as "Påskekrim," a unique Norwegian Easter tradition. Easter eggs and decorations in bright yellow are also common.

Fact 85: Midsummer Celebrations

Midsummer, or "Jonsok," is celebrated around the summer solstice, usually on June 23rd. It is a time to enjoy the long daylight hours and warm weather. Traditional celebrations include lighting bonfires, singing, dancing, and feasting. In some regions, people decorate their homes and barns with flowers and greenery. Midsummer celebrations often reflect Norway's close connection to nature and the seasonal cycles.

Chapter 18: Unique Norwegian Facts

- Fact 86: Midnight Sun

- Fact 87: Northern Lights

- Fact 88: The Nobel Peace Prize

- Fact 89: Hurtigruten Coastal Voyage

- Fact 90: The Svalbard Global Seed Vault

Fact 86: Midnight Sun

The Midnight Sun is a natural phenomenon experienced in Norway during the summer months, especially above the Arctic Circle. From late May to mid-July, the sun does not set, resulting in 24 hours of daylight. This extended daylight period allows for unique experiences like midnight hikes and late-night outdoor activities. The Midnight Sun is a major attraction for tourists visiting northern Norway.

Fact 87: Northern Lights

The Northern Lights, or Aurora Borealis, are a spectacular natural light display that can be seen in northern Norway, particularly in the winter months. These lights are caused by the collision of charged particles from the sun with atoms in the Earth's atmosphere. The result is a stunning array of colors dancing across the night sky. Tromsø and the Lofoten Islands are popular destinations for viewing the Northern Lights.

Fact 88: The Nobel Peace Prize

The Nobel Peace Prize, one of the most prestigious awards in the world, is awarded annually in Oslo, Norway. Established by Alfred Nobel, the inventor of dynamite, the prize honors individuals and organizations that have made significant contributions to peace. The award ceremony takes place on December 10th at the Oslo City Hall and is attended by international dignitaries and laureates.

Fact 89: Hurtigruten Coastal Voyage

The Hurtigruten Coastal Voyage is a famous sea route along Norway's rugged coastline, from Bergen in the south to Kirkenes in the north. Operating since 1893, Hurtigruten ships provide both passenger and freight services, offering breathtaking views of fjords, islands, and coastal towns. The voyage is a popular way for tourists to experience Norway's natural beauty and maritime heritage.

Fact 90: The Svalbard Global Seed Vault

The Svalbard Global Seed Vault, located on the Svalbard archipelago, is a secure seed bank designed to preserve a wide variety of plant seeds. Opened in 2008, it serves as a global insurance policy against the loss of seeds due to catastrophic events. The vault can store up to 4.5 million seed samples, representing a crucial resource for biodiversity and food security. Its remote and cold location ensures the seeds remain viable for long periods.

Chapter 19: Miscellaneous

- Fact 91: Norwegian Folklore

- Fact 92: Famous Norwegian Inventions

- Fact 93: Unique Architectural Styles

-

- Fact 94: Norwegian Work Culture

- Fact 95: Prominent NGOs in Norway

Fact 91: Norwegian Folklore

Norwegian folklore is rich with tales of mythical creatures and supernatural beings. Some of the most well-known figures include trolls, huldra (forest spirits), and Nøkken (a water spirit). These stories, passed down through generations, often feature moral lessons and are deeply intertwined with the country's natural landscapes. Folklore continues to influence Norwegian culture, inspiring art, literature, and festivals.

Fact 92: Famous Norwegian Inventions

Norway has contributed several important inventions to the world. One notable invention is the aerosol spray can, developed by Erik Rotheim in 1926. Another significant Norwegian invention is the paper clip, created by Johan Vaaler in the late 19th century. Norway is also known for advancements in maritime technology and the development of the modern skiing technique by Sondre Norheim.

Fact 93: Unique Architectural Styles

Norway's architectural styles range from traditional wooden stave churches to modern, eco-friendly buildings. Stave churches, such as the one in Borgund, date back to the medieval period and are known for their intricate wood carvings. In contemporary architecture, Norway emphasizes sustainability and innovative design, with buildings like the Oslo Opera House and the energy-positive Powerhouse Brattørkaia in Trondheim.

Fact 94: Norwegian Work Culture

Norwegian work culture is characterized by a strong emphasis on work-life balance and equality. The standard workweek is typically 37.5 hours, and employees enjoy generous vacation time and parental leave. There is a focus on flat organizational structures, open communication, and collaboration. Norwegian workplaces also prioritize employee well-being and offer various benefits to support a healthy work environment.

Fact 95: Prominent NGOs in Norway

Norway is home to several influential non-governmental organizations (NGOs) that work on a variety of global issues. Notable NGOs include the Norwegian Refugee Council, which provides assistance to displaced people worldwide, and Bellona, an environmental organization focused on combating climate change and pollution. These NGOs play a significant role in Norway's commitment to humanitarian aid and environmental protection.

Chapter 20: Future Prospects

- Fact 96: Technological Advancements

- Fact 97: Sustainable Development

- Fact 98: Educational Reforms

- Fact 99: Economic Growth

- Fact 100: Norway's Role in the Global Community

Fact 96: Technological Advancements

Norway is at the forefront of technological advancements, particularly in the fields of renewable energy, maritime technology, and digital innovation. The country invests heavily in research and development to drive technological progress. Norway is also a leader in the adoption of electric vehicles, with significant infrastructure to support their use. Ongoing projects in artificial intelligence, biotechnology, and smart cities promise to shape Norway's future.

Fact 97: Sustainable Development

Norway is dedicated to sustainable development, with ambitious goals to reduce its carbon footprint and protect natural resources. The government has committed to achieving carbon neutrality by 2030 and supports numerous green initiatives, including extensive use of electric vehicles, sustainable farming practices, and renewable energy projects. Norway's approach serves as a model for balancing economic growth with environmental responsibility.

Fact 98: Educational Reforms

Norway continues to implement educational reforms to adapt to the changing needs of society and the global job market. Emphasis is placed on digital literacy, critical thinking, and lifelong learning. The education system is being enhanced to include more interdisciplinary studies and practical skills, ensuring that students are well-prepared for future challenges. Investment in teacher training and educational technology is also a priority.

Fact 99: Economic Growth

Norway's economy is expected to continue growing, driven by sectors such as technology, renewable energy, and sustainable tourism. Diversification efforts are underway to reduce reliance on oil and gas, with a focus on innovation and entrepreneurship. The government's economic policies aim to foster a resilient economy that can withstand global fluctuations and ensure prosperity for future generations.

Fact 100: Norway's Role in the Global Community

Norway plays a significant role in the global community, advocating for peace, sustainability, and human rights. As a member of various international organizations, Norway contributes to global efforts in areas such as climate change mitigation, conflict resolution, and humanitarian aid. The country is committed to being a proactive and responsible global citizen, working collaboratively to address global challenges and promote a better future for all.

Conclusion: Your Norwegian Adventure Awaits!

Wow, young adventurers, you've made it to the end of "100 Amazing Facts About Norway for Young Readers!" From the mystical northern lights to the fearless Viking explorers, you've uncovered so many incredible stories and secrets about this fascinating country.

But remember, this book is just the beginning. Norway is a land full of endless adventures waiting for you to discover. Whether you're dreaming of seeing the majestic fjords, tasting delicious Norwegian waffles, or meeting the friendly people, Norway has so much more to offer.

Keep your spirit of adventure alive, and who knows? Maybe one day, you'll find yourself exploring the wonders of Norway in person. Until then, keep learning, stay curious, and always be ready for your next amazing journey!

Made in United States
North Haven, CT
30 March 2025